50 Greece Sandwich Recipes for Home

By: Kelly Johnson

Table of Contents

- Greek Chicken Souvlaki Pita
- Gyro Sandwich
- Greek Salad Sandwich
- Greek Meatball Pita
- Feta and Olive Tapenade Sandwich
- Tzatziki and Veggie Pita
- Greek Lamb Sandwich
- Spanakopita Wrap
- Greek Chicken and Hummus Wrap
- Greek Tuna Salad Sandwich
- Moussaka Sandwich
- Greek Falafel Pita
- Grilled Halloumi Sandwich
- Greek Eggplant and Feta Wrap
- Lamb Kofta Pita
- Greek Beef Burger
- Saganaki Sandwich
- Greek Shrimp Sandwich
- Pita with Greek Yogurt and Cucumber
- Greek Turkey and Feta Sandwich
- Greek Pork Souvlaki Wrap
- Greek Style Panini
- Greek Avocado and Tomato Sandwich
- Roasted Red Pepper and Feta Sandwich
- Greek Cucumber and Herb Wrap
- Greek Chicken Caesar Sandwich
- Greek Style Grilled Cheese
- Greek Zucchini and Feta Sandwich
- Greek Pork and Pepper Pita
- Greek Egg and Olive Sandwich
- Greek Lentil and Veggie Wrap
- Greek Lamb and Mint Sandwich

- Greek Artichoke and Feta Sandwich
- Greek Mushroom and Spinach Pita
- Greek Roasted Veggie Wrap
- Greek Chicken Shawarma Sandwich
- Greek Tofu and Veggie Pita
- Greek Spicy Sausage Sandwich
- Greek Hummus and Roasted Red Pepper Wrap
- Greek Chickpea and Spinach Pita
- Greek Beef and Tomato Sandwich
- Greek Lamb and Cucumber Wrap
- Greek Chicken and Avocado Sandwich
- Greek Beetroot and Feta Wrap
- Greek Tuna and Olive Sandwich
- Greek Chicken and Feta Pita
- Greek Veggie and Halloumi Wrap
- Greek Lamb and Yogurt Sandwich
- Greek Pita with Grilled Vegetables
- Greek Spiced Beef Wrap

Greek Chicken Souvlaki Pita

Ingredients:

For the Chicken Marinade:

- 500g (1 lb) chicken breast or thighs, cut into bite-sized pieces
- 3 tbsp olive oil
- Juice of 1 lemon
- 3 garlic cloves, minced
- 1 tbsp dried oregano
- 1 tsp ground cumin
- 1 tsp paprika
- Salt and black pepper to taste

For the Tzatziki Sauce:

- 1 cup Greek yogurt
- 1 cucumber, grated and drained
- 2 garlic cloves, minced
- 1 tbsp olive oil
- 1 tbsp lemon juice
- 1 tbsp chopped fresh dill (or 1 tsp dried dill)
- Salt and black pepper to taste

For Assembly:

- 4 pita breads
- 1 cup shredded lettuce
- 1 tomato, sliced
- 1/2 red onion, thinly sliced
- 1/2 cup sliced black olives (optional)
- Fresh parsley for garnish (optional)

Instructions:

1. **Marinate the Chicken:**
    - In a bowl, mix olive oil, lemon juice, garlic, oregano, cumin, paprika, salt, and pepper.
    - Add chicken pieces and toss to coat. Marinate for at least 30 minutes, or up to 4 hours in the refrigerator.
2. **Prepare the Tzatziki Sauce:**
    - In a bowl, combine Greek yogurt, grated cucumber, minced garlic, olive oil, lemon juice, dill, salt, and pepper.

- Mix well and adjust seasoning if needed. Refrigerate until ready to use.
3. **Cook the Chicken:**
    - Preheat a grill or skillet over medium-high heat. If using skewers, thread the marinated chicken onto the skewers.
    - Grill the chicken for about 4-5 minutes per side, or until fully cooked and slightly charred. If using a skillet, cook chicken pieces, turning occasionally until cooked through and golden brown.
4. **Assemble the Pitas:**
    - Warm pita breads in a skillet or oven if desired.
    - Spread a generous amount of tzatziki sauce on each pita.
    - Top with grilled chicken pieces, shredded lettuce, tomato slices, red onion, and olives (if using).
    - Garnish with fresh parsley if desired.
5. **Serve:**
    - Fold the pita around the fillings and serve immediately.

Enjoy your Greek Chicken Souvlaki Pita!

Gyro Sandwich

Ingredients:

For the Gyro Meat:

- 500g (1 lb) ground lamb (or a mix of lamb and beef)
- 1 onion, finely grated
- 3 garlic cloves, minced
- 1 tsp dried oregano
- 1 tsp ground cumin
- 1 tsp ground paprika
- 1/2 tsp ground coriander
- 1/2 tsp ground cinnamon
- Salt and black pepper to taste

For the Tzatziki Sauce:

- 1 cup Greek yogurt
- 1 cucumber, grated and drained
- 2 garlic cloves, minced
- 1 tbsp olive oil
- 1 tbsp lemon juice
- 1 tbsp chopped fresh dill (or 1 tsp dried dill)
- Salt and black pepper to taste

For Assembly:

- 4 pita breads
- 1 cup shredded lettuce
- 1 tomato, sliced
- 1/2 red onion, thinly sliced
- 1/2 cup sliced black olives (optional)
- Fresh parsley for garnish (optional)

Instructions:

1. **Prepare the Gyro Meat:**
    - Preheat your oven to 180°C (350°F).
    - In a bowl, mix ground meat with grated onion, minced garlic, oregano, cumin, paprika, coriander, cinnamon, salt, and pepper.
    - Shape the mixture into a loaf and place it on a baking sheet.
    - Bake for 45-50 minutes, or until fully cooked. Let it rest for 10 minutes before slicing thinly.

2. **Make the Tzatziki Sauce:**
   - Combine Greek yogurt, grated cucumber, minced garlic, olive oil, lemon juice, dill, salt, and pepper in a bowl.
   - Mix well and refrigerate until ready to use.
3. **Assemble the Gyro Sandwich:**
   - Warm pita breads in a skillet or oven.
   - Spread a layer of tzatziki sauce on each pita.
   - Add slices of gyro meat, then top with shredded lettuce, tomato slices, red onion, and olives (if using).
   - Garnish with fresh parsley if desired.
4. **Serve:**
   - Fold the pita around the fillings and enjoy!

This makes for a delicious, authentic Greek gyro sandwich.

Greek Salad Sandwich

Ingredients:

For the Greek Salad:

- 1 cucumber, diced
- 2-3 ripe tomatoes, diced
- 1/2 red onion, thinly sliced
- 1/2 cup Kalamata olives, pitted and halved
- 100g (3.5 oz) feta cheese, crumbled
- 1/4 cup chopped fresh parsley
- 1/4 cup extra-virgin olive oil
- 2 tbsp red wine vinegar
- 1 tsp dried oregano
- Salt and black pepper to taste

For the Sandwich:

- 4 slices of crusty bread (such as ciabatta or baguette)
- 2 tbsp hummus or tzatziki (optional, for spreading)
- 1-2 cups fresh baby spinach or arugula (optional)

Instructions:

1. **Prepare the Greek Salad:**
    - In a large bowl, combine diced cucumber, tomatoes, red onion, Kalamata olives, crumbled feta, and chopped parsley.
    - In a small bowl or jar, whisk together olive oil, red wine vinegar, dried oregano, salt, and pepper.
    - Pour the dressing over the salad and toss gently to combine. Let it sit for a few minutes to allow the flavors to meld.
2. **Prepare the Bread:**
    - If desired, toast the bread slices lightly to add some crunch.
3. **Assemble the Sandwich:**
    - If using, spread a layer of hummus or tzatziki on each slice of bread.
    - Pile the Greek salad mixture onto one slice of bread. Add a handful of baby spinach or arugula if using.
    - Top with another slice of bread to complete the sandwich.
4. **Serve:**
    - Cut the sandwich in half if desired and serve immediately.

This Greek Salad Sandwich is both light and satisfying, perfect for a quick lunch or a healthy snack. Enjoy!

Greek Meatball Pita

Ingredients:

For the Meatballs:

- 500g (1 lb) ground beef or lamb
- 1/2 cup breadcrumbs
- 1/4 cup grated Parmesan cheese
- 1 egg, beaten
- 3 garlic cloves, minced
- 1/4 cup chopped fresh parsley
- 1 tsp dried oregano
- 1/2 tsp ground cumin
- Salt and black pepper to taste

For the Tzatziki Sauce:

- 1 cup Greek yogurt
- 1 cucumber, grated and drained
- 2 garlic cloves, minced
- 1 tbsp olive oil
- 1 tbsp lemon juice
- 1 tbsp chopped fresh dill (or 1 tsp dried dill)
- Salt and black pepper to taste

For Assembly:

- 4 pita breads
- 1 cup shredded lettuce
- 1 tomato, sliced
- 1/2 red onion, thinly sliced
- Fresh parsley for garnish (optional)

Instructions:

1. **Prepare the Meatballs:**
    - Preheat your oven to 180°C (350°F).
    - In a bowl, mix ground meat with breadcrumbs, Parmesan, beaten egg, garlic, parsley, oregano, cumin, salt, and pepper.
    - Shape mixture into small meatballs and place on a baking sheet.
    - Bake for 20-25 minutes, or until meatballs are cooked through and browned.
2. **Make the Tzatziki Sauce:**

- Combine Greek yogurt, grated cucumber, minced garlic, olive oil, lemon juice, dill, salt, and pepper in a bowl.
- Mix well and refrigerate until ready to use.

3. **Assemble the Pitas:**
    - Warm pita breads in a skillet or oven.
    - Spread a layer of tzatziki sauce on each pita.
    - Add the baked meatballs, then top with shredded lettuce, tomato slices, and red onion.
    - Garnish with fresh parsley if desired.
4. **Serve:**
    - Fold the pita around the fillings and serve immediately.

Enjoy your Greek Meatball Pita!

Feta and Olive Tapenade Sandwich

Ingredients:

For the Olive Tapenade:

- 1 cup pitted Kalamata olives
- 1/2 cup green olives
- 2 garlic cloves
- 1/4 cup capers, drained
- 1/4 cup extra-virgin olive oil
- 1 tbsp lemon juice
- 1 tbsp chopped fresh parsley (optional)
- Salt and black pepper to taste

For the Sandwich:

- 4 slices of crusty bread (such as sourdough or ciabatta)
- 100g (3.5 oz) feta cheese, crumbled
- 1/2 cup sun-dried tomatoes, chopped (optional)
- 1 cup fresh spinach or arugula
- 1/2 red onion, thinly sliced (optional)

Instructions:

1. **Prepare the Tapenade:**
   - In a food processor, combine Kalamata olives, green olives, garlic cloves, capers, olive oil, and lemon juice.
   - Pulse until the mixture is finely chopped but still slightly chunky.
   - Stir in chopped parsley if using. Season with salt and pepper to taste.
2. **Prepare the Bread:**
   - Toast the bread slices if desired for added crunch.
3. **Assemble the Sandwich:**
   - Spread a generous amount of olive tapenade on each slice of bread.
   - Top with crumbled feta cheese, sun-dried tomatoes (if using), spinach or arugula, and red onion (if using).
   - Place another slice of bread on top to complete the sandwich.
4. **Serve:**
   - Cut the sandwich in half if desired and serve immediately.

This Feta and Olive Tapenade Sandwich is packed with flavor and makes for a satisfying meal. Enjoy!

Tzatziki and Veggie Pita

Ingredients:

For the Tzatziki Sauce:

- 1 cup Greek yogurt
- 1 cucumber, grated and drained
- 2 garlic cloves, minced
- 1 tbsp olive oil
- 1 tbsp lemon juice
- 1 tbsp chopped fresh dill (or 1 tsp dried dill)
- Salt and black pepper to taste

For the Veggies:

- 1 red bell pepper, sliced
- 1 cucumber, sliced
- 1 carrot, julienned
- 1/2 red onion, thinly sliced
- 1 cup cherry tomatoes, halved
- 1/2 cup Kalamata olives (optional)

For Assembly:

- 4 pita breads
- Fresh parsley for garnish (optional)

Instructions:

1. **Prepare the Tzatziki Sauce:**
   - In a bowl, mix Greek yogurt, grated cucumber, minced garlic, olive oil, lemon juice, dill, salt, and pepper.
   - Stir well and refrigerate until ready to use.
2. **Prepare the Veggies:**
   - Slice and prepare all vegetables. You can either serve them raw or lightly roast them for extra flavor.
3. **Assemble the Pitas:**
   - Warm pita breads in a skillet or oven if desired.
   - Spread a layer of tzatziki sauce inside each pita.
   - Stuff the pitas with sliced bell pepper, cucumber, carrot, red onion, cherry tomatoes, and olives if using.
   - Garnish with fresh parsley if desired.

4. **Serve:**
    - Fold the pita around the fillings and serve immediately.

This Tzatziki and Veggie Pita is fresh, flavorful, and perfect for a light meal. Enjoy!

Greek Lamb Sandwich

Ingredients:

For the Greek Lamb:

- 500g (1 lb) lamb shoulder or leg, thinly sliced
- 3 tbsp olive oil
- Juice of 1 lemon
- 3 garlic cloves, minced
- 1 tbsp dried oregano
- 1 tsp ground cumin
- 1 tsp paprika
- Salt and black pepper to taste

For the Tzatziki Sauce:

- 1 cup Greek yogurt
- 1 cucumber, grated and drained
- 2 garlic cloves, minced
- 1 tbsp olive oil
- 1 tbsp lemon juice
- 1 tbsp chopped fresh dill (or 1 tsp dried dill)
- Salt and black pepper to taste

For the Sandwich:

- 4 pita breads or crusty rolls
- 1 cup shredded lettuce
- 1 tomato, sliced
- 1/2 red onion, thinly sliced
- 1/2 cup Kalamata olives, pitted and sliced (optional)
- Feta cheese, crumbled (optional)

Instructions:

1. **Prepare the Greek Lamb:**
    - In a bowl, mix olive oil, lemon juice, garlic, oregano, cumin, paprika, salt, and pepper.
    - Add the lamb slices and toss to coat well. Marinate for at least 30 minutes or up to 4 hours in the refrigerator.
    - Preheat a grill or skillet over medium-high heat.

- Grill or pan-fry the lamb slices for about 3-4 minutes per side, or until cooked to your desired level of doneness. Let the meat rest for a few minutes before slicing thinly.
2. **Make the Tzatziki Sauce:**
    - In a bowl, combine Greek yogurt, grated cucumber, minced garlic, olive oil, lemon juice, dill, salt, and pepper.
    - Mix well and refrigerate until ready to use.
3. **Assemble the Sandwich:**
    - Warm the pita breads or crusty rolls in a skillet or oven if desired.
    - Spread a generous amount of tzatziki sauce on each pita or roll.
    - Add slices of grilled lamb, then top with shredded lettuce, tomato slices, red onion, olives (if using), and crumbled feta cheese (if using).
4. **Serve:**
    - Fold the pita or top the roll, and serve immediately.

This Greek Lamb Sandwich is packed with flavorful, tender lamb and complemented by the fresh tzatziki sauce. Enjoy!

Spanakopita Wrap

Ingredients:

For the Filling:

- 500g (1 lb) fresh spinach, washed and chopped (or 300g frozen spinach, thawed and drained)
- 200g (7 oz) feta cheese, crumbled
- 1/2 cup ricotta cheese (optional, for added creaminess)
- 1/2 cup finely chopped onions or green onions
- 2-3 garlic cloves, minced
- 1/4 cup fresh dill, chopped (or 1 tbsp dried dill)
- 1/4 cup fresh parsley, chopped
- 2 large eggs, beaten
- Salt and black pepper to taste
- 2 tbsp olive oil (for cooking the filling)

For the Wrap:

- 4 large tortillas or flatbreads
- 1 tbsp olive oil (for brushing the wraps)
- Optional: 1/2 cup grated Parmesan cheese for added flavor

Instructions:

1. **Prepare the Filling:**
    - Heat olive oil in a large skillet over medium heat.
    - Sauté onions and garlic until softened, about 3-4 minutes.
    - Add the spinach and cook until wilted and any excess moisture has evaporated. If using frozen spinach, make sure it's well-drained.
    - Remove from heat and let cool slightly.
    - In a large bowl, combine the spinach mixture with crumbled feta, ricotta (if using), dill, parsley, beaten eggs, salt, and pepper. Mix well.
2. **Assemble the Wraps:**
    - Preheat your oven to 200°C (400°F) if you plan to bake the wraps.
    - Place tortillas or flatbreads on a clean surface. Spread a portion of the spinach filling evenly over each tortilla, leaving a small border around the edges.
    - Roll up the tortillas tightly, folding in the sides as you go, to form a wrap. You can also cut them in half for easier handling if you prefer.
3. **Cook the Wraps:**
    - **Option 1: Bake:** Place the wraps seam-side down on a baking sheet lined with parchment paper. Brush the tops with olive oil and sprinkle with Parmesan

cheese if desired. Bake for 10-15 minutes, or until the wraps are golden and crispy.
- **Option 2: Pan-Fry:** Heat a little olive oil in a skillet over medium heat. Cook the wraps for 2-3 minutes per side, or until golden brown and crispy.
4. **Serve:**
   - Allow the wraps to cool slightly before slicing in half. Serve warm.

These Spanakopita Wraps are a tasty twist on the traditional Greek spinach and feta pie, perfect for a quick lunch or snack. Enjoy!

Greek Chicken and Hummus Wrap

Ingredients:

For the Greek Chicken:

- 500g (1 lb) chicken breast or thighs, thinly sliced
- 3 tbsp olive oil
- Juice of 1 lemon
- 3 garlic cloves, minced
- 1 tbsp dried oregano
- 1 tsp ground cumin
- 1 tsp paprika
- Salt and black pepper to taste

For the Wrap:

- 4 large tortillas or flatbreads
- 1 cup hummus (store-bought or homemade)
- 1 cup shredded lettuce
- 1 tomato, sliced
- 1/2 cucumber, sliced
- 1/2 red onion, thinly sliced
- 1/4 cup Kalamata olives, pitted and sliced (optional)
- 1/4 cup crumbled feta cheese (optional)

Instructions:

1. **Prepare the Greek Chicken:**
   - In a bowl, mix olive oil, lemon juice, garlic, oregano, cumin, paprika, salt, and pepper.
   - Add chicken slices and toss to coat. Marinate for at least 30 minutes or up to 4 hours in the refrigerator.
   - Heat a grill or skillet over medium-high heat. Cook chicken for about 4-5 minutes per side, or until fully cooked and slightly charred. Let rest for a few minutes, then slice thinly.
2. **Assemble the Wraps:**
   - Warm the tortillas or flatbreads in a skillet or oven if desired.
   - Spread a layer of hummus on each tortilla.
   - Layer with shredded lettuce, tomato slices, cucumber slices, red onion, and olives (if using).
   - Top with sliced Greek chicken and crumbled feta cheese (if using).
3. **Wrap and Serve:**
   - Roll up the tortillas tightly, folding in the sides as you go.

- Slice in half if desired and serve immediately.

These Greek Chicken and Hummus Wraps are flavorful and satisfying, making them perfect for a quick meal or lunch. Enjoy!

Greek Tuna Salad Sandwich

Ingredients:

For the Greek Tuna Salad:

- 1 can (185g/6.5 oz) tuna, drained
- 1/4 cup Greek yogurt
- 1 tbsp olive oil
- 1 tbsp lemon juice
- 1 celery stalk, finely chopped
- 1/4 cup red onion, finely chopped
- 1/4 cup Kalamata olives, pitted and sliced
- 1/4 cup crumbled feta cheese
- 1 tbsp fresh parsley, chopped (or 1 tsp dried parsley)
- Salt and black pepper to taste

For the Sandwich:

- 4 slices of bread (whole grain, ciabatta, or your choice)
- 1 cup shredded lettuce
- 1 tomato, sliced
- 1/2 cucumber, sliced

Instructions:

1. **Prepare the Greek Tuna Salad:**
    - In a bowl, combine drained tuna, Greek yogurt, olive oil, lemon juice, celery, red onion, olives, feta cheese, parsley, salt, and pepper.
    - Mix well until all ingredients are evenly combined.
2. **Assemble the Sandwiches:**
    - Spread the tuna salad evenly on two slices of bread.
    - Top with shredded lettuce, tomato slices, and cucumber slices.
    - Place the remaining bread slices on top to complete the sandwich.
3. **Serve:**
    - Cut the sandwiches in half if desired and serve immediately.

This Greek Tuna Salad Sandwich is both refreshing and satisfying, perfect for a light lunch or snack. Enjoy!

Moussaka Sandwich

Ingredients:

For the Moussaka Filling:

- 500g (1 lb) ground beef or lamb
- 1 large eggplant, sliced into 1/4-inch rounds
- 1 large zucchini, sliced into 1/4-inch rounds
- 1 onion, finely chopped
- 2 garlic cloves, minced
- 1 can (400g/14 oz) crushed tomatoes
- 2 tbsp tomato paste
- 1/2 cup red wine (optional)
- 1 tsp dried oregano
- 1/2 tsp ground cinnamon
- 1/2 tsp ground cumin
- 1/4 cup fresh parsley, chopped
- 1/2 cup grated Parmesan cheese
- 1/2 cup béchamel sauce (store-bought or homemade)
- Olive oil for cooking
- Salt and black pepper to taste

For the Sandwich:

- 4 slices of crusty bread (such as ciabatta or sourdough)
- Fresh parsley or basil for garnish (optional)

Instructions:

1. **Prepare the Moussaka Filling:**
    - Preheat your oven to 200°C (400°F).
    - Brush the eggplant and zucchini slices with olive oil and season with salt. Arrange on a baking sheet and roast for 20-25 minutes, or until tender and golden brown. Set aside.
    - In a large skillet, heat a little olive oil over medium heat. Cook the chopped onion until soft, about 5 minutes. Add minced garlic and cook for another minute.
    - Add the ground meat to the skillet and cook until browned. Drain any excess fat.
    - Stir in crushed tomatoes, tomato paste, red wine (if using), oregano, cinnamon, cumin, salt, and pepper. Simmer for 10-15 minutes, until the sauce thickens slightly. Stir in fresh parsley.
    - Remove from heat and let cool slightly.
2. **Assemble the Moussaka Sandwich:**
    - Spread a layer of béchamel sauce on each slice of bread.

        - On two slices of bread, layer roasted eggplant and zucchini slices, followed by a generous portion of the meat sauce.
        - Sprinkle grated Parmesan cheese on top of the meat sauce.
        - Top with the remaining slices of bread.
 3. **Serve:**
        - Optionally, you can toast the assembled sandwiches in a skillet or oven for a crispy exterior and melted cheese.
        - Garnish with fresh parsley or basil if desired.

This Moussaka Sandwich combines the rich flavors of traditional moussaka with the convenience of a sandwich, making it a hearty and flavorful meal. Enjoy!

Greek Falafel Pita

Ingredients:

For the Falafel:

- 1 can (400g/14 oz) chickpeas, drained and rinsed
- 1 small onion, roughly chopped
- 2 garlic cloves
- 1/4 cup fresh parsley, chopped
- 1/4 cup fresh cilantro, chopped
- 1 tsp ground cumin
- 1 tsp ground coriander
- 1/2 tsp baking powder
- Salt and black pepper to taste
- 2-3 tbsp flour (or as needed)
- Olive oil for frying

For the Tzatziki Sauce:

- 1 cup Greek yogurt
- 1 cucumber, grated and drained
- 2 garlic cloves, minced
- 1 tbsp olive oil
- 1 tbsp lemon juice
- 1 tbsp chopped fresh dill (or 1 tsp dried dill)
- Salt and black pepper to taste

For the Pita:

- 4 pita breads
- 1 cup shredded lettuce
- 1 tomato, sliced
- 1/2 cucumber, sliced
- 1/4 red onion, thinly sliced
- 1/4 cup Kalamata olives, pitted and sliced (optional)

Instructions:

1. **Prepare the Falafel:**
    - In a food processor, combine chickpeas, onion, garlic, parsley, cilantro, cumin, coriander, baking powder, salt, and pepper. Process until smooth.
    - Add flour a tablespoon at a time until the mixture holds together but isn't too dry.
    - Shape the mixture into small balls or patties.

- Heat olive oil in a skillet over medium heat. Fry the falafel in batches, turning occasionally, until golden brown and crispy, about 3-4 minutes per side. Drain on paper towels.
2. **Make the Tzatziki Sauce:**
    - In a bowl, mix Greek yogurt, grated cucumber, minced garlic, olive oil, lemon juice, dill, salt, and pepper.
    - Stir well and refrigerate until ready to use.
3. **Assemble the Pitas:**
    - Warm the pita breads in a skillet or oven.
    - Spread a generous amount of tzatziki sauce inside each pita.
    - Stuff with shredded lettuce, tomato slices, cucumber slices, red onion, and Kalamata olives (if using).
    - Add a few falafel balls or patties to each pita.
4. **Serve:**
    - Fold the pita around the fillings and serve immediately.

This Greek Falafel Pita is a flavorful and satisfying vegetarian option, perfect for a quick meal or lunch. Enjoy!

Grilled Halloumi Sandwich

Ingredients:

For the Sandwich:

- 200g (7 oz) halloumi cheese, sliced into 1/2-inch thick slices
- 4 slices of crusty bread (such as ciabatta or sourdough)
- 2 tbsp olive oil
- 1 ripe tomato, sliced
- 1/2 cucumber, sliced
- 1/4 red onion, thinly sliced
- 1/2 avocado, sliced (optional)
- Fresh basil or arugula for garnish (optional)
- Salt and black pepper to taste

For the Dressing (optional):

- 2 tbsp olive oil
- 1 tbsp balsamic vinegar or lemon juice
- 1 tsp Dijon mustard
- 1 tsp honey or maple syrup
- Salt and black pepper to taste

Instructions:

1. **Grill the Halloumi:**
   - Heat olive oil in a grill pan or skillet over medium-high heat.
   - Grill the halloumi slices for about 2-3 minutes per side, or until golden brown and crispy. Remove from heat and set aside.
2. **Prepare the Dressing (optional):**
   - In a small bowl, whisk together olive oil, balsamic vinegar or lemon juice, Dijon mustard, honey, salt, and pepper.
3. **Assemble the Sandwiches:**
   - Toast the bread slices if desired.
   - Place grilled halloumi slices on two of the bread slices.
   - Top with tomato slices, cucumber slices, red onion, and avocado (if using).
   - Drizzle with the optional dressing if desired.
   - Add fresh basil or arugula for garnish, then top with the remaining bread slices.
4. **Serve:**
   - Cut the sandwiches in half if desired and serve immediately.

This Grilled Halloumi Sandwich is flavorful and satisfying, combining the rich taste of halloumi with fresh vegetables. Enjoy!

Greek Eggplant and Feta Wrap

Ingredients:

For the Filling:

- 1 large eggplant, cut into 1/2-inch cubes
- 2 tbsp olive oil
- 1 tsp dried oregano
- 1/2 tsp ground cumin
- Salt and black pepper to taste
- 100g (3.5 oz) feta cheese, crumbled
- 1/4 cup Kalamata olives, pitted and sliced
- 1/4 cup sun-dried tomatoes, chopped (optional)
- 1/4 cup fresh parsley, chopped

For the Wrap:

- 4 large tortillas or flatbreads
- 1 cup shredded lettuce or baby spinach
- 1 tomato, sliced
- 1/2 cucumber, sliced
- 1/2 red onion, thinly sliced
- 1/2 cup tzatziki sauce (store-bought or homemade)

Instructions:

1. **Prepare the Eggplant:**
    - Preheat your oven to 200°C (400°F).
    - Toss eggplant cubes with olive oil, oregano, cumin, salt, and pepper. Spread on a baking sheet.
    - Roast for 20-25 minutes, or until eggplant is tender and golden brown. Let cool slightly.
2. **Assemble the Wraps:**
    - Warm the tortillas or flatbreads in a skillet or oven.
    - Spread a layer of tzatziki sauce on each tortilla.
    - Top with shredded lettuce or baby spinach, roasted eggplant, crumbled feta, olives, sun-dried tomatoes (if using), and fresh parsley.
    - Add tomato slices, cucumber slices, and red onion.
3. **Wrap and Serve:**
    - Fold the sides of the tortilla over the filling and roll up tightly.
    - Cut in half if desired and serve immediately.

This Greek Eggplant and Feta Wrap is packed with flavor and perfect for a light and satisfying meal. Enjoy!

Lamb Kofta Pita

Ingredients:

For the Lamb Kofta:

- 500g (1 lb) ground lamb
- 1/4 cup fresh parsley, chopped
- 1/4 cup fresh cilantro, chopped
- 1 onion, finely chopped
- 3 garlic cloves, minced
- 1 tsp ground cumin
- 1 tsp ground coriander
- 1 tsp smoked paprika
- 1/2 tsp ground cinnamon
- 1/2 tsp ground allspice
- Salt and black pepper to taste

For the Tzatziki Sauce:

- 1 cup Greek yogurt
- 1 cucumber, grated and drained
- 2 garlic cloves, minced
- 1 tbsp olive oil
- 1 tbsp lemon juice
- 1 tbsp chopped fresh dill (or 1 tsp dried dill)
- Salt and black pepper to taste

For the Pita:

- 4 pita breads
- 1 cup shredded lettuce
- 1 tomato, sliced
- 1/2 cucumber, sliced
- 1/4 red onion, thinly sliced
- Fresh parsley or mint for garnish (optional)

Instructions:

1. **Prepare the Lamb Kofta:**
    - In a large bowl, combine ground lamb with parsley, cilantro, onion, garlic, cumin, coriander, paprika, cinnamon, allspice, salt, and pepper.
    - Mix well until fully combined.
    - Shape the mixture into small oval or cylindrical patties.

- Heat a grill or skillet over medium-high heat. Cook kofta patties for about 3-4 minutes per side, or until fully cooked and browned.
2. **Make the Tzatziki Sauce:**
    - In a bowl, mix Greek yogurt, grated cucumber, minced garlic, olive oil, lemon juice, dill, salt, and pepper.
    - Stir well and refrigerate until ready to use.
3. **Assemble the Pitas:**
    - Warm the pita breads in a skillet or oven.
    - Spread a layer of tzatziki sauce inside each pita.
    - Add shredded lettuce, tomato slices, cucumber slices, and red onion.
    - Place 2-3 kofta patties into each pita.
4. **Serve:**
    - Garnish with fresh parsley or mint if desired, and serve immediately.

This Lamb Kofta Pita is flavorful and makes for a delicious, satisfying meal. Enjoy!

Greek Beef Burger

Ingredients:

For the Greek Beef Patties:

- 500g (1 lb) ground beef
- 1/4 cup feta cheese, crumbled
- 1/4 cup Kalamata olives, pitted and chopped
- 2 garlic cloves, minced
- 1/4 cup fresh parsley, chopped
- 1 tbsp dried oregano
- 1/2 tsp ground cumin
- Salt and black pepper to taste

For the Tzatziki Sauce:

- 1 cup Greek yogurt
- 1 cucumber, grated and drained
- 2 garlic cloves, minced
- 1 tbsp olive oil
- 1 tbsp lemon juice
- 1 tbsp chopped fresh dill (or 1 tsp dried dill)
- Salt and black pepper to taste

For Assembly:

- 4 burger buns
- 1 cup shredded lettuce
- 1 tomato, sliced
- 1/2 red onion, sliced
- Fresh dill or parsley for garnish (optional)

Instructions:

1. **Prepare the Greek Beef Patties:**
   - In a bowl, combine ground beef, feta cheese, olives, garlic, parsley, oregano, cumin, salt, and pepper. Mix until just combined.
   - Shape the mixture into 4 patties.
   - Heat a grill or skillet over medium-high heat. Cook patties for about 4-5 minutes per side, or until they reach your desired level of doneness.
2. **Make the Tzatziki Sauce:**
   - In a bowl, mix Greek yogurt, grated cucumber, minced garlic, olive oil, lemon juice, dill, salt, and pepper.

- Stir well and refrigerate until ready to use.
3. **Assemble the Burgers:**
    - Toast the burger buns if desired.
    - Spread a generous amount of tzatziki sauce on the bottom half of each bun.
    - Place a cooked beef patty on each bun, then top with shredded lettuce, tomato slices, and red onion.
    - Garnish with fresh dill or parsley if desired. Place the top bun on each burger.
4. **Serve:**
    - Serve the burgers immediately and enjoy!

These Greek Beef Burgers are packed with Mediterranean flavors and are perfect for a delicious and satisfying meal.

Saganaki Sandwich

Ingredients:

For the Saganaki:

- 200g (7 oz) kasseri or halloumi cheese, sliced into 1/2-inch thick slices
- 1/4 cup all-purpose flour (for coating)
- 1 egg, beaten (for coating)
- 1/4 cup breadcrumbs (optional, for extra crispiness)
- Olive oil for frying

For the Sandwich:

- 4 slices of crusty bread (such as ciabatta or sourdough)
- 1/2 cup tzatziki sauce (store-bought or homemade)
- 1 tomato, sliced
- 1/2 cucumber, sliced
- 1/4 red onion, thinly sliced
- Fresh basil or parsley for garnish (optional)

Instructions:

1. **Prepare the Saganaki:**
    - Coat each cheese slice in flour, shaking off excess.
    - Dip in beaten egg, allowing excess to drip off.
    - Optionally, coat with breadcrumbs for extra crispiness.
    - Heat olive oil in a skillet over medium-high heat. Fry cheese slices for 2-3 minutes per side, or until golden brown and crispy. Remove from the skillet and drain on paper towels.
2. **Assemble the Sandwiches:**
    - Toast the bread slices if desired.
    - Spread a layer of tzatziki sauce on each slice of bread.
    - Place a fried saganaki slice on each of two bread slices.
    - Top with tomato slices, cucumber slices, and red onion.
    - Garnish with fresh basil or parsley if desired.
3. **Serve:**
    - Top with the remaining bread slices to complete the sandwich and serve immediately.

This Saganaki Sandwich features crispy, gooey cheese and fresh vegetables, offering a delicious Mediterranean twist. Enjoy!

Greek Shrimp Sandwich

Ingredients:

For the Greek Shrimp:

- 500g (1 lb) large shrimp, peeled and deveined
- 2 tbsp olive oil
- 2 garlic cloves, minced
- 1 tsp dried oregano
- 1/2 tsp ground cumin
- 1/2 tsp paprika
- 1 tbsp lemon juice
- Salt and black pepper to taste

For the Tzatziki Sauce:

- 1 cup Greek yogurt
- 1 cucumber, grated and drained
- 2 garlic cloves, minced
- 1 tbsp olive oil
- 1 tbsp lemon juice
- 1 tbsp chopped fresh dill (or 1 tsp dried dill)
- Salt and black pepper to taste

For the Sandwich:

- 4 pita breads or crusty rolls
- 1 cup shredded lettuce
- 1 tomato, sliced
- 1/2 cucumber, sliced
- 1/4 red onion, thinly sliced
- Fresh parsley for garnish (optional)

Instructions:

1. **Prepare the Greek Shrimp:**
   - In a bowl, mix olive oil, garlic, oregano, cumin, paprika, lemon juice, salt, and pepper.
   - Add shrimp and toss to coat. Marinate for 15-30 minutes.
   - Heat a skillet over medium-high heat. Cook shrimp for 2-3 minutes per side, or until pink and cooked through. Remove from heat.
2. **Make the Tzatziki Sauce:**

- In a bowl, combine Greek yogurt, grated cucumber, minced garlic, olive oil, lemon juice, dill, salt, and pepper.
- Stir well and refrigerate until ready to use.
3. **Assemble the Sandwiches:**
    - Warm the pita breads or rolls in a skillet or oven.
    - Spread a generous amount of tzatziki sauce inside each pita or roll.
    - Add shredded lettuce, tomato slices, cucumber slices, and red onion.
    - Top with cooked shrimp.
4. **Serve:**
    - Garnish with fresh parsley if desired and serve immediately.

This Greek Shrimp Sandwich is fresh, flavorful, and perfect for a light yet satisfying meal. Enjoy!

Pita with Greek Yogurt and Cucumber

Ingredients:

For the Greek Yogurt Spread:

- 1 cup Greek yogurt
- 1 cucumber, grated and excess moisture squeezed out
- 2 garlic cloves, minced
- 1 tbsp olive oil
- 1 tbsp lemon juice
- 1 tbsp fresh dill, chopped (or 1 tsp dried dill)
- Salt and black pepper to taste

For the Pita:

- 4 pita breads
- Fresh herbs for garnish (optional, such as dill or parsley)

Instructions:

1. **Prepare the Greek Yogurt Spread:**
   - In a bowl, combine Greek yogurt, grated cucumber, minced garlic, olive oil, lemon juice, dill, salt, and pepper.
   - Mix well until all ingredients are fully incorporated.
   - Taste and adjust seasoning as needed.
2. **Warm the Pita:**
   - Heat pita breads in a skillet or oven until warm and soft.
3. **Assemble the Pita:**
   - Cut each pita in half to create pockets (or use whole if preferred).
   - Spread a generous amount of the Greek yogurt mixture inside each pita pocket or on top of each whole pita.
4. **Serve:**
   - Garnish with additional fresh herbs if desired.
   - Serve immediately, either as a light meal, snack, or side dish.

This Pita with Greek Yogurt and Cucumber is refreshing and versatile, making it a great option for a quick meal or appetizer. Enjoy!

Greek Turkey and Feta Sandwich

Ingredients:

For the Greek Turkey Filling:

- 250g (8 oz) cooked turkey breast, sliced or shredded
- 1/4 cup crumbled feta cheese
- 1/4 cup Kalamata olives, pitted and sliced
- 1/4 cup sun-dried tomatoes, chopped
- 2 tbsp fresh parsley, chopped
- 1 tsp dried oregano
- 1 tbsp olive oil
- 1 tbsp lemon juice
- Salt and black pepper to taste

For the Sandwich:

- 4 slices of crusty bread (such as ciabatta or sourdough)
- 1 cup shredded lettuce
- 1 tomato, sliced
- 1/2 cucumber, sliced
- 1/4 red onion, thinly sliced
- Fresh basil or arugula for garnish (optional)

Instructions:

1. **Prepare the Greek Turkey Filling:**
    - In a bowl, combine the cooked turkey, crumbled feta cheese, Kalamata olives, sun-dried tomatoes, parsley, oregano, olive oil, and lemon juice.
    - Mix well to combine all ingredients.
    - Season with salt and black pepper to taste.
2. **Assemble the Sandwiches:**
    - Toast the bread slices if desired.
    - Spread a layer of the Greek turkey filling evenly over two slices of bread.
    - Top with shredded lettuce, tomato slices, cucumber slices, and red onion.
    - Garnish with fresh basil or arugula if desired.
    - Place the remaining slices of bread on top to complete the sandwich.
3. **Serve:**
    - Cut the sandwiches in half if desired and serve immediately.

This Greek Turkey and Feta Sandwich is packed with Mediterranean flavors and makes for a hearty and satisfying meal. Enjoy!

Greek Pork Souvlaki Wrap

Ingredients:

For the Pork Souvlaki:

- 500g (1 lb) pork tenderloin or pork shoulder, cut into 1-inch cubes
- 3 tbsp olive oil
- Juice of 1 lemon
- 3 garlic cloves, minced
- 1 tbsp dried oregano
- 1 tsp ground cumin
- 1 tsp paprika
- Salt and black pepper to taste

For the Tzatziki Sauce:

- 1 cup Greek yogurt
- 1 cucumber, grated and drained
- 2 garlic cloves, minced
- 1 tbsp olive oil
- 1 tbsp lemon juice
- 1 tbsp chopped fresh dill (or 1 tsp dried dill)
- Salt and black pepper to taste

For the Wrap:

- 4 large tortillas or flatbreads
- 1 cup shredded lettuce
- 1 tomato, sliced
- 1/2 cucumber, sliced
- 1/4 red onion, thinly sliced
- Fresh parsley or mint for garnish (optional)

Instructions:

1. **Prepare the Pork Souvlaki:**
   - In a bowl, combine olive oil, lemon juice, garlic, oregano, cumin, paprika, salt, and pepper.
   - Add pork cubes and toss to coat. Marinate for at least 30 minutes or up to 4 hours in the refrigerator.
   - Heat a grill or skillet over medium-high heat. Cook pork cubes for about 8-10 minutes, turning occasionally, until fully cooked and slightly charred. Remove from heat.

2. **Make the Tzatziki Sauce:**
    - In a bowl, mix Greek yogurt, grated cucumber, minced garlic, olive oil, lemon juice, dill, salt, and pepper.
    - Stir well and refrigerate until ready to use.
3. **Assemble the Wraps:**
    - Warm the tortillas or flatbreads in a skillet or oven.
    - Spread a layer of tzatziki sauce on each tortilla.
    - Top with shredded lettuce, tomato slices, cucumber slices, and red onion.
    - Add a generous portion of grilled pork souvlaki.
4. **Wrap and Serve:**
    - Fold in the sides of the tortilla and roll up tightly.
    - Slice in half if desired and garnish with fresh parsley or mint.
    - Serve immediately.

This Greek Pork Souvlaki Wrap is flavorful and satisfying, making it a perfect choice for a delicious meal or lunch. Enjoy!

Greek Style Panini

Ingredients:

For the Panini:

- 4 ciabatta rolls or other crusty bread rolls
- 200g (7 oz) sliced cooked chicken breast or rotisserie chicken
- 1/4 cup crumbled feta cheese
- 1/4 cup Kalamata olives, pitted and sliced
- 1/2 cup roasted red peppers, sliced
- 1/4 cup sliced red onion
- 1 cup fresh spinach or arugula
- 2 tbsp olive tapenade (optional)
- 2 tbsp olive oil
- Salt and black pepper to taste

Instructions:

1. **Prepare the Ingredients:**
   - Slice the ciabatta rolls in half horizontally.
   - If using olive tapenade, spread a layer on the inside of each bread roll.
2. **Assemble the Panini:**
   - On the bottom half of each ciabatta roll, layer the cooked chicken, crumbled feta cheese, Kalamata olives, roasted red peppers, and sliced red onion.
   - Top with fresh spinach or arugula.
   - Drizzle with a little olive oil and season with salt and black pepper if needed.
3. **Grill the Panini:**
   - Heat a panini press or grill pan over medium heat.
   - Brush the outside of the ciabatta rolls with olive oil.
   - Place the sandwiches in the panini press or on the grill pan. If using a grill pan, press down with a heavy skillet or pan to flatten the sandwiches.
   - Grill for about 3-4 minutes, or until the bread is golden and crispy and the cheese is melted.
4. **Serve:**
   - Remove from heat and let cool slightly before slicing in half if desired.
   - Serve immediately.

This Greek Style Panini combines Mediterranean flavors with the satisfying crunch of a grilled sandwich. Enjoy!

Greek Avocado and Tomato Sandwich

Ingredients:

For the Sandwich:

- 2 ripe avocados, peeled and sliced
- 2 large tomatoes, sliced
- 1/4 cup crumbled feta cheese
- 1/4 cup Kalamata olives, pitted and sliced
- 1/4 red onion, thinly sliced
- 1/2 cup fresh basil leaves
- 4 slices of crusty bread (such as ciabatta or sourdough)
- 2 tbsp olive oil
- 1 tbsp lemon juice
- Salt and black pepper to taste

Optional for Extra Flavor:

- 1/2 tsp dried oregano
- 1 clove garlic, minced

Instructions:

1. **Prepare the Ingredients:**
   - In a small bowl, mix olive oil, lemon juice, minced garlic (if using), salt, and pepper.
   - Brush or drizzle this mixture on one side of each slice of bread.
2. **Assemble the Sandwiches:**
   - Layer avocado slices on two of the bread slices.
   - Top with tomato slices, crumbled feta cheese, Kalamata olives, and red onion.
   - Sprinkle with dried oregano if desired.
   - Add fresh basil leaves on top.
3. **Finish the Sandwich:**
   - Place the remaining bread slices on top to complete the sandwiches.
   - Optionally, you can toast the sandwiches in a skillet or oven for added crispiness.
4. **Serve:**
   - Cut in half if desired and serve immediately.

This Greek Avocado and Tomato Sandwich is light, fresh, and full of Mediterranean flavors. Enjoy!

Roasted Red Pepper and Feta Sandwich

Ingredients:

For the Sandwich:

- 4 slices of crusty bread (such as ciabatta, sourdough, or a baguette)
- 1 jar (about 1 cup) roasted red peppers, drained and sliced
- 100g (3.5 oz) feta cheese, crumbled
- 1/4 cup Kalamata olives, pitted and sliced (optional)
- 1/4 red onion, thinly sliced
- 1/2 cup fresh spinach or arugula
- 2 tbsp olive oil
- 1 tbsp balsamic vinegar
- Salt and black pepper to taste

Optional for Extra Flavor:

- 1 tsp dried oregano or fresh basil
- 1 garlic clove, minced

Instructions:

1. **Prepare the Ingredients:**
   - In a small bowl, mix olive oil, balsamic vinegar, and minced garlic (if using). Brush this mixture lightly on one side of each slice of bread.
   - Season with salt and black pepper.
2. **Assemble the Sandwiches:**
   - Place the bread slices on a work surface, oil side up.
   - On two of the bread slices, layer roasted red peppers, crumbled feta cheese, Kalamata olives (if using), red onion slices, and fresh spinach or arugula.
   - Sprinkle with dried oregano or fresh basil if desired.
3. **Finish the Sandwich:**
   - Top with the remaining bread slices.
   - Optionally, you can toast the sandwiches in a skillet or oven for a crispy texture.
4. **Serve:**
   - Cut the sandwiches in half if desired and serve immediately.

This Roasted Red Pepper and Feta Sandwich is a flavorful combination of tangy feta and sweet roasted peppers, perfect for a satisfying meal. Enjoy!

Greek Cucumber and Herb Wrap

Ingredients:

For the Wrap Filling:

- 1 large cucumber, sliced or julienned
- 1 cup Greek yogurt
- 2 tbsp fresh dill, chopped (or 1 tsp dried dill)
- 2 tbsp fresh mint, chopped (or 1 tsp dried mint)
- 2 tbsp fresh parsley, chopped
- 1 garlic clove, minced
- 1 tbsp lemon juice
- Salt and black pepper to taste

For the Wrap:

- 4 large tortillas or flatbreads
- 1 cup shredded lettuce
- 1 tomato, sliced
- 1/4 red onion, thinly sliced
- 1/4 cup Kalamata olives, pitted and sliced (optional)
- 1/4 cup crumbled feta cheese (optional)

Instructions:

1. **Prepare the Greek Cucumber and Herb Mixture:**
   - In a bowl, combine Greek yogurt, dill, mint, parsley, minced garlic, lemon juice, salt, and black pepper.
   - Stir in cucumber slices or julienned cucumber. Mix until well coated.
2. **Assemble the Wraps:**
   - Warm the tortillas or flatbreads in a skillet or oven.
   - Spread a generous layer of the cucumber and herb mixture down the center of each tortilla.
   - Top with shredded lettuce, tomato slices, red onion, and Kalamata olives (if using).
   - Sprinkle with crumbled feta cheese if desired.
3. **Wrap and Serve:**
   - Fold in the sides of the tortilla and roll up tightly to enclose the filling.
   - Slice in half if desired and serve immediately.

This Greek Cucumber and Herb Wrap is light, fresh, and packed with flavor, making it a perfect choice for a quick and satisfying meal. Enjoy!

Greek Chicken Caesar Sandwich

Ingredients:

For the Greek Chicken:

- 500g (1 lb) chicken breast, cooked and sliced
- 2 tbsp olive oil
- 1 tbsp lemon juice
- 1 tsp dried oregano
- 1 tsp garlic powder
- Salt and black pepper to taste

For the Caesar Dressing:

- 1/2 cup Greek yogurt
- 1/4 cup grated Parmesan cheese
- 1 tbsp lemon juice
- 1 garlic clove, minced
- 1 tsp Dijon mustard
- Salt and black pepper to taste

For the Sandwich:

- 4 slices of crusty bread (such as ciabatta or sourdough)
- 1 cup romaine lettuce, chopped
- 1/4 cup cherry tomatoes, halved
- 1/4 cup sliced Kalamata olives (optional)
- Extra grated Parmesan for garnish (optional)

Instructions:

1. **Prepare the Greek Chicken:**
   - In a bowl, combine olive oil, lemon juice, oregano, garlic powder, salt, and pepper.
   - Toss the sliced chicken in the mixture until well coated.
   - Heat a skillet over medium-high heat and cook the chicken slices for 2-3 minutes per side, or until warmed through.
2. **Make the Caesar Dressing:**
   - In a bowl, mix Greek yogurt, grated Parmesan cheese, lemon juice, minced garlic, Dijon mustard, salt, and pepper.
   - Stir until smooth and well combined.
3. **Assemble the Sandwiches:**
   - Toast the bread slices if desired.

        - Spread a layer of Caesar dressing on each slice of bread.
        - Layer the cooked chicken slices on two of the bread slices.
        - Top with chopped romaine lettuce, cherry tomatoes, and Kalamata olives if using.
        - Sprinkle with extra Parmesan cheese if desired.
4. **Finish and Serve:**
        - Top with the remaining bread slices to complete the sandwich.
        - Cut in half if desired and serve immediately.

This Greek Chicken Caesar Sandwich is a delicious twist on the classic Caesar, combining Greek flavors with a hearty sandwich. Enjoy!

Greek Style Grilled Cheese

Ingredients:

For the Sandwich:

- 4 slices of crusty bread (such as sourdough or ciabatta)
- 100g (3.5 oz) feta cheese, crumbled
- 100g (3.5 oz) kasseri or mozzarella cheese, sliced
- 1/4 cup Kalamata olives, pitted and sliced
- 1/4 cup roasted red peppers, sliced
- 1/4 red onion, thinly sliced
- 1 tbsp fresh oregano, chopped (or 1 tsp dried oregano)
- 2 tbsp olive oil or butter for grilling

Instructions:

1. **Prepare the Ingredients:**
   - Preheat a skillet or griddle over medium heat.
   - If using fresh oregano, chop it finely.
2. **Assemble the Sandwiches:**
   - On two slices of bread, layer the kasseri or mozzarella cheese, crumbled feta, Kalamata olives, roasted red peppers, and red onion.
   - Sprinkle with chopped oregano.
   - Top with the remaining slices of bread.
3. **Grill the Sandwiches:**
   - Brush or spread olive oil or butter on the outside of each slice of bread.
   - Place the sandwiches in the preheated skillet or griddle.
   - Grill for 3-4 minutes per side, or until the bread is golden brown and the cheese is melted.
4. **Serve:**
   - Remove from heat and let cool for a minute before cutting in half.
   - Serve immediately.

This Greek Style Grilled Cheese combines Mediterranean flavors with the classic comfort of a grilled cheese sandwich. Enjoy!

Greek Zucchini and Feta Sandwich

Ingredients:

For the Sandwich:

- 2 medium zucchinis, sliced into thin rounds or half-moons
- 1/4 cup crumbled feta cheese
- 1/4 cup Kalamata olives, pitted and sliced
- 1/4 red onion, thinly sliced
- 1/2 cup fresh spinach or arugula
- 4 slices of crusty bread (such as ciabatta or sourdough)
- 2 tbsp olive oil
- 1 tbsp lemon juice
- 1 tsp dried oregano
- Salt and black pepper to taste

Optional for Extra Flavor:

- 1 garlic clove, minced
- 1 tbsp balsamic glaze or vinegar

Instructions:

1. **Prepare the Zucchini:**
   - Heat 1 tbsp of olive oil in a skillet over medium heat.
   - Add the sliced zucchini and cook for about 4-5 minutes per side, or until tender and lightly browned.
   - Season with salt, pepper, and dried oregano. Add minced garlic if desired.
   - Remove from heat and let cool slightly.
2. **Assemble the Sandwiches:**
   - Brush the remaining 1 tbsp of olive oil on one side of each bread slice.
   - Optionally, toast the bread slices in the skillet or oven until golden brown.
   - On the non-oiled side of two slices of bread, layer the cooked zucchini, crumbled feta cheese, Kalamata olives, red onion, and fresh spinach or arugula.
   - Drizzle with lemon juice and balsamic glaze or vinegar if using.
3. **Finish the Sandwich:**
   - Top with the remaining bread slices, oiled side up.
   - Press down slightly and optionally grill in a skillet for about 2 minutes per side until the bread is golden and the cheese is slightly melted.
4. **Serve:**
   - Cut in half if desired and serve immediately.

This Greek Zucchini and Feta Sandwich is a flavorful and light option, perfect for a satisfying meal or a tasty lunch. Enjoy!

Greek Pork and Pepper Pita

Ingredients:

For the Greek Pork:

- 500g (1 lb) pork tenderloin or pork shoulder, thinly sliced
- 2 tbsp olive oil
- 1 tbsp lemon juice
- 1 tbsp dried oregano
- 2 garlic cloves, minced
- 1 tsp paprika
- Salt and black pepper to taste

For the Pita Filling:

- 1 red bell pepper, sliced
- 1 yellow bell pepper, sliced
- 1/2 red onion, sliced
- 1/4 cup crumbled feta cheese
- 1/4 cup Kalamata olives, pitted and sliced (optional)
- 1/2 cup tzatziki sauce (store-bought or homemade)

For the Pita Bread:

- 4 pita breads

Instructions:

1. **Prepare the Greek Pork:**
    - In a bowl, mix olive oil, lemon juice, oregano, garlic, paprika, salt, and pepper.
    - Toss the pork slices in the marinade and let sit for at least 30 minutes.
    - Heat a skillet over medium-high heat and cook the pork for about 4-5 minutes per side, or until fully cooked and slightly crispy. Remove from heat.
2. **Cook the Peppers and Onions:**
    - In the same skillet, add a bit more olive oil if needed and sauté the bell peppers and red onion for about 5-7 minutes, or until tender and slightly caramelized. Season with a pinch of salt and pepper.
3. **Assemble the Pita:**
    - Warm the pita breads in a skillet or oven until soft.
    - Spread a layer of tzatziki sauce inside each pita.
    - Fill with the cooked pork, sautéed peppers and onions, crumbled feta cheese, and Kalamata olives if using.
4. **Serve:**

- Fold the pita to enclose the filling and serve immediately.

This Greek Pork and Pepper Pita is full of Mediterranean flavors and perfect for a quick and satisfying meal. Enjoy!

Greek Egg and Olive Sandwich

Ingredients:

For the Filling:

- 4 hard-boiled eggs, peeled and chopped
- 1/4 cup Kalamata olives, pitted and chopped
- 2 tbsp Greek yogurt
- 1 tbsp mayonnaise (optional)
- 1 tbsp fresh dill or parsley, chopped
- 1 tbsp lemon juice
- Salt and black pepper to taste

For the Sandwich:

- 4 slices of crusty bread (such as ciabatta, sourdough, or whole grain)
- 1 cup fresh spinach or arugula
- 1 tomato, sliced
- 1/4 red onion, thinly sliced

Instructions:

1. **Prepare the Filling:**
   - In a bowl, combine chopped hard-boiled eggs, Kalamata olives, Greek yogurt, mayonnaise (if using), fresh dill or parsley, lemon juice, salt, and pepper.
   - Mix gently until well combined.
2. **Assemble the Sandwiches:**
   - Toast the bread slices if desired.
   - Spread a layer of the egg and olive mixture on two of the bread slices.
   - Top with fresh spinach or arugula, tomato slices, and red onion.
   - Place the remaining bread slices on top to complete the sandwiches.
3. **Serve:**
   - Cut in half if desired and serve immediately.

This Greek Egg and Olive Sandwich offers a flavorful twist on the classic egg salad, perfect for a light and satisfying meal. Enjoy!

Greek Lentil and Veggie Wrap

Ingredients:

For the Lentil Filling:

- 1 cup cooked lentils (green or brown)
- 1 tbsp olive oil
- 1 garlic clove, minced
- 1/2 red bell pepper, diced
- 1/2 zucchini, diced
- 1/2 cup cherry tomatoes, halved
- 1/4 cup Kalamata olives, pitted and sliced
- 1 tsp dried oregano
- 1/2 tsp ground cumin
- Salt and black pepper to taste

For the Wrap:

- 4 large tortillas or flatbreads
- 1 cup fresh spinach or arugula
- 1/4 cup crumbled feta cheese
- 1/4 cup tzatziki sauce (store-bought or homemade)

Instructions:

1. **Prepare the Lentil Filling:**
   - Heat olive oil in a skillet over medium heat.
   - Add minced garlic and sauté for 1 minute.
   - Add diced red bell pepper and zucchini, and cook for 4-5 minutes until tender.
   - Stir in cherry tomatoes, Kalamata olives, dried oregano, ground cumin, salt, and pepper.
   - Add cooked lentils and cook for an additional 2-3 minutes, until heated through. Remove from heat.
2. **Assemble the Wraps:**
   - Warm the tortillas or flatbreads in a skillet or oven.
   - Spread a layer of tzatziki sauce on each tortilla.
   - Add a layer of fresh spinach or arugula.
   - Top with the lentil and veggie mixture.
   - Sprinkle with crumbled feta cheese.
3. **Wrap and Serve:**
   - Fold in the sides of the tortilla and roll up tightly to enclose the filling.
   - Slice in half if desired and serve immediately.

This Greek Lentil and Veggie Wrap is hearty and packed with Mediterranean flavors, making it a nutritious and satisfying meal. Enjoy!

Greek Lamb and Mint Sandwich

Ingredients:

For the Greek Lamb:

- 500g (1 lb) lamb shoulder or lamb loin, sliced thinly
- 2 tbsp olive oil
- 2 tbsp fresh mint, chopped (or 1 tbsp dried mint)
- 2 garlic cloves, minced
- 1 tbsp lemon juice
- 1 tsp dried oregano
- 1 tsp ground cumin
- Salt and black pepper to taste

For the Sandwich:

- 4 pita breads or crusty rolls (like ciabatta or baguette)
- 1/2 cup tzatziki sauce (store-bought or homemade)
- 1 cup shredded lettuce
- 1 tomato, sliced
- 1/2 cucumber, sliced
- 1/4 red onion, thinly sliced
- Fresh mint leaves for garnish

Instructions:

1. **Prepare the Greek Lamb:**
   - In a bowl, mix olive oil, chopped mint, minced garlic, lemon juice, oregano, cumin, salt, and pepper.
   - Add the lamb slices and toss to coat thoroughly. Marinate for at least 30 minutes or up to 4 hours in the refrigerator.
   - Heat a skillet or grill pan over medium-high heat. Cook the lamb slices for about 3-4 minutes per side, or until cooked to your desired doneness. Remove from heat and let rest.
2. **Assemble the Sandwiches:**
   - Warm the pita breads or rolls in a skillet or oven.
   - Spread a layer of tzatziki sauce on each pita or roll.
   - Add a layer of shredded lettuce, followed by tomato slices, cucumber slices, and red onion.
   - Top with the cooked lamb slices.
   - Garnish with fresh mint leaves.
3. **Serve:**
   - Cut the sandwiches in half if desired and serve immediately.

This Greek Lamb and Mint Sandwich is flavorful and aromatic, perfect for a delicious and satisfying meal. Enjoy!

Greek Artichoke and Feta Sandwich

Ingredients:

For the Sandwich:

- 1 cup marinated artichoke hearts, drained and chopped
- 100g (3.5 oz) crumbled feta cheese
- 1/4 cup Kalamata olives, pitted and sliced
- 1/4 cup roasted red peppers, sliced
- 1/4 red onion, thinly sliced
- 1 tbsp fresh basil or parsley, chopped
- 2 tbsp olive oil
- 1 tbsp lemon juice
- Salt and black pepper to taste

For the Sandwich:

- 4 slices of crusty bread (such as ciabatta, sourdough, or a baguette)
- 1 cup fresh spinach or arugula

Instructions:

1. **Prepare the Artichoke Mixture:**
   - In a bowl, combine chopped artichoke hearts, crumbled feta cheese, Kalamata olives, roasted red peppers, red onion, and fresh basil or parsley.
   - Drizzle with olive oil and lemon juice. Season with salt and black pepper. Mix well.
2. **Assemble the Sandwiches:**
   - Toast the bread slices if desired.
   - Layer fresh spinach or arugula on two of the bread slices.
   - Spoon the artichoke and feta mixture on top of the spinach.
   - Top with the remaining bread slices to complete the sandwiches.
3. **Serve:**
   - Cut the sandwiches in half if desired and serve immediately.

This Greek Artichoke and Feta Sandwich is flavorful and packed with Mediterranean ingredients, perfect for a fresh and satisfying meal. Enjoy!

Greek Mushroom and Spinach Pita

Ingredients:

For the Filling:

- 2 cups fresh spinach, chopped
- 1 cup mushrooms, sliced (such as cremini or button)
- 1 tbsp olive oil
- 1 garlic clove, minced
- 1/4 cup crumbled feta cheese
- 1/4 cup Kalamata olives, pitted and sliced (optional)
- 1/4 tsp dried oregano
- Salt and black pepper to taste

For the Pita:

- 4 pita breads

Instructions:

1. **Prepare the Filling:**
   - Heat olive oil in a skillet over medium heat.
   - Add minced garlic and sauté for 1 minute.
   - Add sliced mushrooms and cook for about 5-7 minutes, until tender and browned.
   - Stir in the chopped spinach and cook until wilted, about 2 minutes.
   - Remove from heat and mix in crumbled feta cheese, Kalamata olives (if using), dried oregano, salt, and pepper.
2. **Assemble the Pitas:**
   - Warm the pita breads in a skillet or oven.
   - Cut or gently open the pitas to form pockets if they aren't pre-split.
   - Fill each pita with the mushroom and spinach mixture.
3. **Serve:**
   - Serve immediately, or warm the stuffed pitas briefly in the oven to melt the feta slightly.

This Greek Mushroom and Spinach Pita is a delicious and easy way to enjoy Mediterranean flavors in a handheld form. Enjoy!

Greek Roasted Veggie Wrap

Ingredients:

For the Roasted Veggies:

- 1 red bell pepper, sliced
- 1 zucchini, sliced
- 1 red onion, sliced
- 1 cup cherry tomatoes, halved
- 2 tbsp olive oil
- 1 tsp dried oregano
- 1/2 tsp garlic powder
- Salt and black pepper to taste

For the Wrap:

- 4 large tortillas or flatbreads
- 1/2 cup crumbled feta cheese
- 1/2 cup hummus (store-bought or homemade)
- 1/4 cup Kalamata olives, pitted and sliced (optional)
- 1 cup fresh spinach or arugula
- 1/4 cup sliced red onion (optional)

Instructions:

1. **Roast the Veggies:**
    - Preheat the oven to 400°F (200°C).
    - Toss the red bell pepper, zucchini, red onion, and cherry tomatoes with olive oil, dried oregano, garlic powder, salt, and black pepper.
    - Spread the veggies on a baking sheet in a single layer.
    - Roast for 20-25 minutes, or until tender and slightly caramelized. Remove from oven and let cool slightly.
2. **Assemble the Wraps:**
    - Warm the tortillas or flatbreads in a skillet or oven.
    - Spread a layer of hummus on each tortilla.
    - Add a layer of roasted veggies, crumbled feta cheese, Kalamata olives (if using), and fresh spinach or arugula.
    - Optionally, add sliced red onion.
3. **Wrap and Serve:**
    - Fold in the sides of the tortilla and roll up tightly to enclose the filling.
    - Slice in half if desired and serve immediately.

This Greek Roasted Veggie Wrap is vibrant, flavorful, and perfect for a nutritious meal on the go. Enjoy!

Greek Chicken Shawarma Sandwich

Ingredients:

For the Chicken Shawarma:

- 500g (1 lb) chicken thighs, boneless and skinless
- 2 tbsp olive oil
- 2 tbsp Greek yogurt
- 2 tbsp lemon juice
- 1 tbsp ground cumin
- 1 tbsp ground coriander
- 1 tsp paprika
- 1 tsp ground turmeric
- 1 tsp ground cinnamon
- 1/2 tsp ground allspice
- 3 garlic cloves, minced
- 1 tsp dried oregano
- Salt and black pepper to taste

For the Sandwich:

- 4 pita breads or flatbreads
- 1/2 cup tzatziki sauce (store-bought or homemade)
- 1 cup shredded lettuce
- 1 tomato, sliced
- 1/2 cucumber, sliced
- 1/4 red onion, thinly sliced
- Fresh parsley for garnish (optional)

Instructions:

1. **Prepare the Chicken Shawarma:**
   - In a bowl, combine olive oil, Greek yogurt, lemon juice, cumin, coriander, paprika, turmeric, cinnamon, allspice, minced garlic, dried oregano, salt, and black pepper.
   - Add the chicken thighs and coat well with the marinade. Cover and refrigerate for at least 1 hour, preferably overnight for best results.
2. **Cook the Chicken:**
   - Preheat a grill, grill pan, or skillet over medium-high heat.
   - Grill or cook the marinated chicken thighs for about 6-8 minutes per side, or until fully cooked and slightly charred. The internal temperature should reach 165°F (74°C).
   - Remove from heat and let the chicken rest for a few minutes before slicing into strips.
3. **Assemble the Sandwiches:**
   - Warm the pita breads or flatbreads in a skillet or oven.

        - Spread a layer of tzatziki sauce on each pita or flatbread.
        - Add shredded lettuce, tomato slices, cucumber slices, and red onion.
        - Top with the sliced chicken shawarma.
        - Garnish with fresh parsley if desired.
    4. **Serve:**
        - Fold or wrap the pita around the filling and serve immediately.

This Greek Chicken Shawarma Sandwich is flavorful and satisfying, combining the savory spices of shawarma with fresh, crisp vegetables. Enjoy!

Greek Tofu and Veggie Pita

Ingredients:

For the Greek Tofu:

- 400g (14 oz) firm tofu, drained and pressed
- 2 tbsp olive oil
- 1 tbsp lemon juice
- 1 tsp dried oregano
- 1 tsp dried basil
- 1/2 tsp garlic powder
- 1/2 tsp paprika
- Salt and black pepper to taste

For the Veggies:

- 1 red bell pepper, sliced
- 1 zucchini, sliced
- 1/2 red onion, sliced
- 1 tbsp olive oil
- 1/2 tsp dried oregano
- Salt and black pepper to taste

For the Pita:

- 4 pita breads
- 1/2 cup tzatziki sauce (store-bought or homemade)
- 1/2 cup crumbled feta cheese (optional)
- 1 cup fresh spinach or arugula
- 1/4 cup Kalamata olives, pitted and sliced (optional)

Instructions:

1. **Prepare the Greek Tofu:**
    - Cut the tofu into bite-sized cubes.
    - In a bowl, mix olive oil, lemon juice, dried oregano, dried basil, garlic powder, paprika, salt, and black pepper.
    - Toss the tofu cubes in the marinade and let sit for at least 15 minutes.
    - Heat a skillet over medium-high heat and cook the marinated tofu for 5-7 minutes, turning occasionally, until golden brown and crispy on all sides. Remove from heat.
2. **Cook the Veggies:**
    - Heat olive oil in a skillet over medium heat.
    - Add sliced red bell pepper, zucchini, and red onion. Cook for about 5-7 minutes, or until tender and slightly caramelized.
    - Season with dried oregano, salt, and black pepper.

3. **Assemble the Pitas:**
    - Warm the pita breads in a skillet or oven.
    - Spread a layer of tzatziki sauce inside each pita.
    - Add a layer of fresh spinach or arugula.
    - Fill with the cooked tofu and sautéed veggies.
    - Optionally, sprinkle with crumbled feta cheese and Kalamata olives.
4. **Serve:**
    - Fold the pita to enclose the filling and serve immediately.

This Greek Tofu and Veggie Pita is a flavorful and satisfying meal, offering a great combination of Mediterranean flavors with a hearty plant-based twist. Enjoy!

Greek Spicy Sausage Sandwich

Ingredients:

For the Greek Spicy Sausage:

- 500g (1 lb) spicy Greek sausage (such as loukaniko or a similar variety), sliced into 1/4-inch rounds
- 1 tbsp olive oil
- 1/2 tsp dried oregano
- 1/2 tsp paprika
- 1/4 tsp red pepper flakes (adjust based on heat preference)

For the Sandwich:

- 4 crusty rolls or ciabatta bread
- 1/2 cup tzatziki sauce (store-bought or homemade)
- 1/2 cup crumbled feta cheese
- 1 cup shredded lettuce
- 1 tomato, sliced
- 1/2 cucumber, sliced
- 1/4 red onion, thinly sliced
- 1/4 cup Kalamata olives, pitted and sliced (optional)

Instructions:

1. **Prepare the Sausage:**
   - Heat olive oil in a skillet over medium heat.
   - Add the sliced sausage and cook for about 5-7 minutes, or until browned and cooked through.
   - Sprinkle with dried oregano, paprika, and red pepper flakes during the last 2 minutes of cooking.
2. **Assemble the Sandwiches:**
   - Warm the rolls or ciabatta bread in a skillet or oven.
   - Spread a layer of tzatziki sauce on the inside of each roll.
   - Add a layer of shredded lettuce, followed by tomato slices, cucumber slices, and red onion.
   - Top with the cooked spicy sausage.
   - Optionally, sprinkle with crumbled feta cheese and Kalamata olives.
3. **Serve:**
   - Close the sandwiches with the top half of the rolls.
   - Cut in half if desired and serve immediately.

This Greek Spicy Sausage Sandwich is flavorful and hearty, combining the spiciness of the sausage with refreshing Mediterranean ingredients. Enjoy!

Greek Hummus and Roasted Red Pepper Wrap

Ingredients:

For the Wrap:

- 4 large tortillas or flatbreads
- 1 cup hummus (store-bought or homemade)
- 1 cup roasted red peppers, sliced (from a jar or homemade)
- 1/2 cup crumbled feta cheese
- 1/2 cup Kalamata olives, pitted and sliced
- 1 cup fresh spinach or arugula
- 1/4 red onion, thinly sliced
- 1/4 cup fresh basil or parsley, chopped (optional)

Instructions:

1. **Prepare the Wrap Ingredients:**
    - If using store-bought roasted red peppers, drain and slice them into strips.
    - Warm the tortillas or flatbreads in a skillet or oven until pliable.
2. **Assemble the Wraps:**
    - Spread a generous layer of hummus on each tortilla.
    - Layer roasted red peppers, crumbled feta cheese, Kalamata olives, fresh spinach or arugula, and sliced red onion on top of the hummus.
    - Optionally, add fresh basil or parsley for extra flavor.
3. **Wrap and Serve:**
    - Fold in the sides of the tortilla and roll it up tightly to enclose the filling.
    - Slice in half if desired and serve immediately.

This Greek Hummus and Roasted Red Pepper Wrap is fresh, flavorful, and perfect for a quick and satisfying meal. Enjoy!

Greek Chickpea and Spinach Pita

Ingredients:

For the Chickpea Filling:

- 1 can (15 oz) chickpeas, drained and rinsed
- 1 tbsp olive oil
- 2 garlic cloves, minced
- 1/2 tsp ground cumin
- 1/2 tsp paprika
- 1/4 tsp ground coriander
- 1/2 tsp dried oregano
- Salt and black pepper to taste
- 1 cup fresh spinach, chopped
- 1/4 cup crumbled feta cheese

For the Pita:

- 4 pita breads
- 1/2 cup tzatziki sauce (store-bought or homemade)
- 1/4 cup Kalamata olives, pitted and sliced (optional)
- 1/2 cucumber, sliced
- 1 tomato, sliced

Instructions:

1. **Prepare the Chickpea Filling:**
    - Heat olive oil in a skillet over medium heat.
    - Add minced garlic and sauté for about 1 minute until fragrant.
    - Add chickpeas and cook for 5-7 minutes, stirring occasionally, until they start to crisp up and become golden.
    - Stir in ground cumin, paprika, ground coriander, dried oregano, salt, and pepper.
    - Add chopped spinach and cook for another 2 minutes, until the spinach is wilted and mixed in.
    - Remove from heat and gently stir in crumbled feta cheese.
2. **Assemble the Pitas:**
    - Warm the pita breads in a skillet or oven until soft and pliable.
    - Spread a layer of tzatziki sauce inside each pita.
    - Fill with the chickpea and spinach mixture.
    - Optionally, add sliced Kalamata olives, cucumber slices, and tomato slices.
3. **Serve:**
    - Fold the pita to enclose the filling and serve immediately.

This Greek Chickpea and Spinach Pita is flavorful and packed with nutritious ingredients, making it a satisfying and delicious meal. Enjoy!

Greek Beef and Tomato Sandwich

Ingredients:

For the Beef:

- 500g (1 lb) beef sirloin or flank steak, thinly sliced
- 2 tbsp olive oil
- 1 tbsp lemon juice
- 1 tbsp dried oregano
- 1 tsp garlic powder
- 1/2 tsp paprika
- Salt and black pepper to taste

For the Sandwich:

- 4 slices of crusty bread (such as ciabatta, sourdough, or baguette)
- 1/2 cup tzatziki sauce (store-bought or homemade)
- 1 large tomato, sliced
- 1/4 red onion, thinly sliced
- 1/4 cup Kalamata olives, pitted and sliced (optional)
- Fresh basil or parsley for garnish (optional)

Instructions:

1. **Prepare the Beef:**
   - In a bowl, mix olive oil, lemon juice, dried oregano, garlic powder, paprika, salt, and black pepper.
   - Toss the thinly sliced beef in the marinade, making sure each piece is well coated. Let marinate for at least 30 minutes or up to 4 hours in the refrigerator.
   - Heat a skillet over medium-high heat. Cook the beef slices for about 2-3 minutes per side, or until cooked to your desired level of doneness. Remove from heat and let rest.
2. **Assemble the Sandwiches:**
   - Toast the bread slices if desired.
   - Spread a layer of tzatziki sauce on each slice of bread.
   - Layer with tomato slices, red onion slices, and Kalamata olives if using.
   - Top with the cooked beef slices.
   - Garnish with fresh basil or parsley if desired.
3. **Serve:**
   - Place the remaining bread slices on top to complete the sandwiches.
   - Cut in half if desired and serve immediately.

This Greek Beef and Tomato Sandwich combines tender, marinated beef with fresh, Mediterranean flavors for a delicious and satisfying meal. Enjoy!

Greek Lamb and Cucumber Wrap

Ingredients:

For the Greek Lamb:

- 500g (1 lb) lamb shoulder or lamb loin, thinly sliced
- 2 tbsp olive oil
- 2 tbsp lemon juice
- 1 tbsp dried oregano
- 1 tsp ground cumin
- 1 tsp garlic powder
- 1/2 tsp paprika
- Salt and black pepper to taste

For the Wrap:

- 4 large tortillas or flatbreads
- 1/2 cup tzatziki sauce (store-bought or homemade)
- 1 cup fresh spinach or arugula
- 1/2 cucumber, sliced into thin rounds
- 1/2 red onion, thinly sliced
- 1/4 cup crumbled feta cheese (optional)
- Fresh dill or mint for garnish (optional)

Instructions:

1. **Prepare the Greek Lamb:**
   - In a bowl, mix olive oil, lemon juice, dried oregano, ground cumin, garlic powder, paprika, salt, and black pepper.
   - Toss the lamb slices in the marinade and let sit for at least 30 minutes or up to 4 hours in the refrigerator.
   - Heat a skillet or grill pan over medium-high heat. Cook the lamb slices for about 4-5 minutes per side, or until cooked to your desired level of doneness. Remove from heat and let rest for a few minutes.
2. **Assemble the Wraps:**
   - Warm the tortillas or flatbreads in a skillet or oven until soft.
   - Spread a layer of tzatziki sauce on each tortilla.
   - Add a layer of fresh spinach or arugula.
   - Top with sliced cucumber, red onion, and the cooked lamb slices.
   - Optionally, sprinkle with crumbled feta cheese and garnish with fresh dill or mint.
3. **Wrap and Serve:**
   - Fold in the sides of the tortilla and roll up tightly to enclose the filling.
   - Slice in half if desired and serve immediately.

This Greek Lamb and Cucumber Wrap is full of Mediterranean flavors, offering a fresh and satisfying meal that's easy to enjoy on the go.

Greek Chicken and Avocado Sandwich

Ingredients:

For the Greek Chicken:

- 500g (1 lb) chicken breast or thighs, boneless and skinless
- 2 tbsp olive oil
- 2 tbsp Greek yogurt
- 1 tbsp lemon juice
- 1 tbsp dried oregano
- 1 tsp garlic powder
- 1/2 tsp paprika
- Salt and black pepper to taste

For the Sandwich:

- 4 slices of crusty bread (such as ciabatta, sourdough, or baguette)
- 1 ripe avocado, sliced
- 1/2 cup tzatziki sauce (store-bought or homemade)
- 1 cup fresh spinach or arugula
- 1 tomato, sliced
- 1/4 red onion, thinly sliced
- Fresh parsley or dill for garnish (optional)

Instructions:

1. **Prepare the Greek Chicken:**
     - In a bowl, mix olive oil, Greek yogurt, lemon juice, dried oregano, garlic powder, paprika, salt, and black pepper.
     - Coat the chicken pieces with the marinade and let sit for at least 30 minutes or up to 4 hours in the refrigerator.
     - Preheat a grill or skillet over medium-high heat.
     - Cook the chicken for 5-7 minutes per side, or until fully cooked and the internal temperature reaches 165°F (74°C). Let the chicken rest for a few minutes, then slice into strips.
2. **Assemble the Sandwiches:**
     - Toast the bread slices if desired.
     - Spread a layer of tzatziki sauce on each slice of bread.
     - Add a layer of sliced avocado on two of the bread slices.
     - Top with sliced chicken, fresh spinach or arugula, tomato slices, and red onion.
     - Garnish with fresh parsley or dill if desired.
3. **Serve:**
     - Place the remaining bread slices on top to complete the sandwiches.
     - Cut in half if desired and serve immediately.

This Greek Chicken and Avocado Sandwich is packed with flavors and textures, combining tender marinated chicken with creamy avocado and fresh vegetables. Enjoy!

Greek Beetroot and Feta Wrap

Ingredients:

For the Wrap:

- 1 cup cooked beetroot, sliced or cubed (fresh or pre-cooked)
- 1/2 cup crumbled feta cheese
- 1/4 cup Kalamata olives, pitted and sliced
- 1/2 red onion, thinly sliced
- 1 cup fresh spinach or arugula
- 2 tbsp olive oil
- 1 tbsp lemon juice
- 1 tsp dried oregano
- Salt and black pepper to taste

For the Wrap:

- 4 large tortillas or flatbreads

Instructions:

1. **Prepare the Beetroot:**
   - If using fresh beetroot, peel and cook it until tender (boil or roast), then slice or cube.
   - In a bowl, toss the beetroot with olive oil, lemon juice, dried oregano, salt, and black pepper.
2. **Assemble the Wraps:**
   - Warm the tortillas or flatbreads in a skillet or oven until soft.
   - Layer fresh spinach or arugula on each tortilla.
   - Top with the seasoned beetroot, crumbled feta cheese, Kalamata olives, and sliced red onion.
3. **Wrap and Serve:**
   - Fold in the sides of the tortilla and roll up tightly to enclose the filling.
   - Slice in half if desired and serve immediately.

This Greek Beetroot and Feta Wrap is vibrant and full of flavor, combining earthy beetroot with tangy feta and fresh greens for a delicious and nutritious meal. Enjoy!

Greek Tuna and Olive Sandwich

Ingredients:

For the Tuna Mixture:

- 1 can (5 oz) tuna in olive oil, drained
- 1/4 cup Kalamata olives, pitted and sliced
- 2 tbsp capers, rinsed and drained
- 1/4 cup red onion, finely chopped
- 2 tbsp fresh parsley or dill, chopped
- 1 tbsp lemon juice
- 2 tbsp Greek yogurt or mayonnaise
- Salt and black pepper to taste

For the Sandwich:

- 4 slices of crusty bread (such as ciabatta, sourdough, or baguette)
- 1 cup fresh spinach or arugula
- 1 tomato, sliced
- 1/2 cucumber, sliced
- 1/4 cup crumbled feta cheese (optional)

Instructions:

1. **Prepare the Tuna Mixture:**
   - In a bowl, combine the drained tuna, Kalamata olives, capers, red onion, parsley or dill, lemon juice, and Greek yogurt or mayonnaise.
   - Mix until well combined. Season with salt and black pepper to taste.
2. **Assemble the Sandwiches:**
   - Toast the bread slices if desired.
   - Spread a layer of the tuna mixture on two slices of bread.
   - Top with fresh spinach or arugula, tomato slices, and cucumber slices.
   - Optionally, sprinkle with crumbled feta cheese.
3. **Serve:**
   - Place the remaining bread slices on top to complete the sandwiches.
   - Cut in half if desired and serve immediately.

This Greek Tuna and Olive Sandwich combines savory tuna with tangy olives and fresh vegetables for a flavorful and satisfying meal. Enjoy!

Greek Chicken and Feta Pita

Ingredients:

For the Greek Chicken:

- 500g (1 lb) chicken breast or thighs, boneless and skinless
- 2 tbsp olive oil
- 2 tbsp Greek yogurt
- 1 tbsp lemon juice
- 1 tbsp dried oregano
- 1 tsp garlic powder
- 1/2 tsp paprika
- Salt and black pepper to taste

For the Pita:

- 4 pita breads
- 1/2 cup crumbled feta cheese
- 1/2 cup tzatziki sauce (store-bought or homemade)
- 1 cup fresh spinach or arugula
- 1 tomato, sliced
- 1/2 cucumber, sliced
- 1/4 red onion, thinly sliced
- Fresh parsley or dill for garnish (optional)

Instructions:

1. **Prepare the Greek Chicken:**
   - In a bowl, mix olive oil, Greek yogurt, lemon juice, dried oregano, garlic powder, paprika, salt, and black pepper.
   - Coat the chicken pieces with the marinade and let sit for at least 30 minutes or up to 4 hours in the refrigerator.
   - Preheat a grill, grill pan, or skillet over medium-high heat.
   - Cook the chicken for about 5-7 minutes per side, or until fully cooked and the internal temperature reaches 165°F (74°C). Let the chicken rest for a few minutes before slicing into strips.
2. **Assemble the Pitas:**
   - Warm the pita breads in a skillet or oven until soft and pliable.
   - Spread a layer of tzatziki sauce inside each pita.
   - Add a layer of fresh spinach or arugula.
   - Fill with sliced chicken, crumbled feta cheese, tomato slices, cucumber slices, and red onion.
   - Garnish with fresh parsley or dill if desired.
3. **Serve:**
   - Fold the pita to enclose the filling and serve immediately.

This Greek Chicken and Feta Pita is packed with Mediterranean flavors and is both fresh and satisfying. Enjoy!

Greek Veggie and Halloumi Wrap

Ingredients:

For the Veggies:

- 1 red bell pepper, sliced
- 1 zucchini, sliced
- 1/2 red onion, sliced
- 1 tbsp olive oil
- 1/2 tsp dried oregano
- Salt and black pepper to taste

For the Halloumi:

- 200g (7 oz) halloumi cheese, sliced
- 1 tbsp olive oil

For the Wrap:

- 4 large tortillas or flatbreads
- 1/2 cup tzatziki sauce (store-bought or homemade)
- 1 cup fresh spinach or arugula
- 1/2 cucumber, sliced
- 1 tomato, sliced
- Fresh parsley or dill for garnish (optional)

Instructions:

1. **Prepare the Veggies:**
   - Preheat the oven to 400°F (200°C).
   - Toss the red bell pepper, zucchini, and red onion with olive oil, dried oregano, salt, and black pepper.
   - Spread on a baking sheet and roast for 20-25 minutes, or until tender and slightly caramelized.
2. **Cook the Halloumi:**
   - Heat olive oil in a skillet over medium heat.
   - Cook the halloumi slices for about 2-3 minutes per side, until golden brown and crispy.
3. **Assemble the Wraps:**
   - Warm the tortillas or flatbreads in a skillet or oven until soft.
   - Spread a layer of tzatziki sauce on each tortilla.
   - Add a layer of fresh spinach or arugula.
   - Top with roasted veggies, cooked halloumi, cucumber slices, and tomato slices.
   - Garnish with fresh parsley or dill if desired.
4. **Wrap and Serve:**
   - Fold in the sides of the tortilla and roll up tightly to enclose the filling.
   - Slice in half if desired and serve immediately.

This Greek Veggie and Halloumi Wrap is deliciously satisfying, combining the creamy halloumi with roasted vegetables and fresh ingredients. Enjoy!

Greek Lamb and Yogurt Sandwich

Ingredients:

For the Greek Lamb:

- 500g (1 lb) lamb shoulder or lamb loin, thinly sliced
- 2 tbsp olive oil
- 2 tbsp Greek yogurt
- 1 tbsp lemon juice
- 1 tbsp dried oregano
- 1 tsp ground cumin
- 1 tsp garlic powder
- 1/2 tsp paprika
- Salt and black pepper to taste

For the Sandwich:

- 4 slices of crusty bread (such as ciabatta, sourdough, or baguette)
- 1/2 cup Greek yogurt
- 1 tbsp lemon juice
- 1 garlic clove, minced
- 1/2 cucumber, sliced
- 1 tomato, sliced
- 1/4 red onion, thinly sliced
- Fresh mint or parsley for garnish (optional)

Instructions:

1. **Prepare the Greek Lamb:**
   - In a bowl, mix olive oil, Greek yogurt, lemon juice, dried oregano, ground cumin, garlic powder, paprika, salt, and black pepper.
   - Coat the lamb slices with the marinade and let sit for at least 30 minutes or up to 4 hours in the refrigerator.
   - Heat a grill, grill pan, or skillet over medium-high heat.
   - Cook the lamb slices for about 4-5 minutes per side, or until cooked to your desired level of doneness. Remove from heat and let rest for a few minutes.
2. **Prepare the Yogurt Sauce:**
   - In a small bowl, mix Greek yogurt with lemon juice and minced garlic. Season with a pinch of salt and pepper.
3. **Assemble the Sandwiches:**
   - Toast the bread slices if desired.
   - Spread a layer of the yogurt sauce on each slice of bread.
   - Layer with the cooked lamb slices, cucumber, tomato, and red onion.
   - Garnish with fresh mint or parsley if desired.
4. **Serve:**
   - Place the remaining bread slices on top to complete the sandwiches.
   - Cut in half if desired and serve immediately.

This Greek Lamb and Yogurt Sandwich combines tender marinated lamb with a refreshing yogurt sauce and fresh vegetables for a flavorful and satisfying meal. Enjoy!

Greek Pita with Grilled Vegetables

Ingredients:

For the Grilled Vegetables:

- 1 red bell pepper, sliced
- 1 zucchini, sliced
- 1 eggplant, sliced
- 1/2 red onion, sliced
- 2 tbsp olive oil
- 1 tsp dried oregano
- Salt and black pepper to taste

For the Pita:

- 4 pita breads
- 1/2 cup hummus (store-bought or homemade)
- 1/4 cup crumbled feta cheese
- 1/4 cup Kalamata olives, pitted and sliced
- 1 cup fresh spinach or arugula
- 1/2 cucumber, sliced
- 1 tomato, sliced

Instructions:

1. **Prepare the Grilled Vegetables:**
   - Preheat your grill or grill pan to medium-high heat.
   - Toss the red bell pepper, zucchini, eggplant, and red onion with olive oil, dried oregano, salt, and black pepper.
   - Grill the vegetables for about 4-5 minutes per side, or until tender and charred. Remove from heat and set aside.
2. **Assemble the Pitas:**
   - Warm the pita breads in a skillet or oven until soft.
   - Spread a layer of hummus inside each pita.
   - Fill with the grilled vegetables, crumbled feta cheese, and Kalamata olives.
   - Add fresh spinach or arugula, cucumber slices, and tomato slices.
3. **Serve:**
   - Fold the pita to enclose the filling and serve immediately.

This Greek Pita with Grilled Vegetables is fresh and full of Mediterranean flavors, making it a delicious and satisfying option for lunch or dinner. Enjoy!

Greek Spiced Beef Wrap

Ingredients:

For the Greek Spiced Beef:

- 500g (1 lb) beef sirloin or flank steak, thinly sliced
- 2 tbsp olive oil
- 2 tbsp Greek yogurt
- 1 tbsp lemon juice
- 1 tbsp dried oregano
- 1 tsp ground cumin
- 1 tsp paprika
- 1/2 tsp ground cinnamon
- 1/2 tsp garlic powder
- 1/4 tsp ground coriander
- Salt and black pepper to taste

For the Wrap:

- 4 large tortillas or flatbreads
- 1/2 cup tzatziki sauce (store-bought or homemade)
- 1 cup fresh spinach or arugula
- 1/2 cucumber, sliced
- 1 tomato, sliced
- 1/4 red onion, thinly sliced
- 1/4 cup crumbled feta cheese (optional)
- Fresh parsley or dill for garnish (optional)

Instructions:

1. **Prepare the Greek Spiced Beef:**
   - In a bowl, mix olive oil, Greek yogurt, lemon juice, dried oregano, ground cumin, paprika, ground cinnamon, garlic powder, ground coriander, salt, and black pepper.
   - Toss the beef slices in the marinade and let sit for at least 30 minutes or up to 4 hours in the refrigerator.
   - Heat a grill, grill pan, or skillet over medium-high heat.
   - Cook the beef slices for about 2-3 minutes per side, or until cooked to your desired level of doneness. Remove from heat and let rest for a few minutes before slicing into strips.
2. **Assemble the Wraps:**
   - Warm the tortillas or flatbreads in a skillet or oven until soft.
   - Spread a layer of tzatziki sauce on each tortilla.
   - Add a layer of fresh spinach or arugula.
   - Top with the spiced beef slices, cucumber, tomato, and red onion.
   - Optionally, sprinkle with crumbled feta cheese and garnish with fresh parsley or dill.
3. **Wrap and Serve:**
   - Fold in the sides of the tortilla and roll up tightly to enclose the filling.
   - Slice in half if desired and serve immediately.

This Greek Spiced Beef Wrap offers a flavorful combination of spiced beef with fresh vegetables and creamy tzatziki, making it a satisfying and delicious meal. Enjoy!